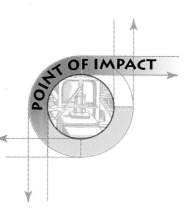

POINT OF IMPACT

The Printing Press

A Breakthrough in Communication

RICHARD TAMES

Heinemann Library
Chicago, Illinois

© 2001 Reed Educational & Professional Publishing
Published by Heinemann Library,
an imprint of Reed Educational & Professional Publishing,
100 N. LaSalle, Suite 1010
Chicago, IL 60602
Customer Service 888-454-2279
Visit our website at www.heinemannlibrary.com

Designed by Robert Sydenham, Ambassador Design Ltd, Bristol.
Originated by Ambassador Litho, Bristol.
Printed in Hong Kong

05 04 03 02 01
10 9 8 7 6 5 4 3 2 1

Library of Congress Cataloging-in-Publication Data
Tames, Richard.
    Printing press : a breakthrough in communication / Richard Tames.
        p. cm. – (Point of impact)
    Includes bibliographical references and index.
    Summary: Surveys the development of the printing press, from advances in Asia and Gutenberg's work in Germany to the profound impact of printing on civilization in general.
    ISBN 1-57572-418-9 (library binding)
    1. Printing—History—Juvenile literature. [1. Printing—History.]. I. Title. II. Series.

Z124 .T36 2000
686.2—dc21

00-026084

Acknowledgments
The Publishers would like to thank the following for permission to reproduce photographs: Bridgeman, p. 9, p. 6 (British Library), p. 5 (Christie's), p. 11 (The Stapleton Collection), p. 8 (Trinity College); Corbis, pp. 18, 21, 28, p. 14 (Michael Maslan), p. 4 (Underwood & Underwood); Mary Evans Picture Library, pp. 7, 12; National Maritime Museum, p. 15; Richard Tames, pp. 19, 22, 23, 26; The British Library, pp. 10, 20; University of Reading Library, pp. 16, 17; Victoria and Albert Museum, p. 13.

Cover photograph reproduced with permission of Corbis (Bettmann).

Our thanks to Christopher Gibb for his help in the preparation of this book.

Some words are shown in bold, **like this.** You can find out what they mean by looking in the glossary.

16.95

Contents

Made in Mainz

Man with a mission

Johann Gutenberg (about 1398–1468) spent his life on a great project, only to see his dream fulfilled by his own business partner, rather than himself. In Gutenberg's time, books were copied slowly, by hand. This made them incredibly expensive. Gutenberg noticed that Europeans used carved wooden blocks to print playing cards or souvenir pictures of saints. They used presses to crush grapes for their juice. Gutenberg combined these basic processes, adding other ideas to create a whole new printing technology. He wanted to produce whole books, printed from separate pieces of metal **type** that, unlike carved blocks, could be broken down and used again.

A replica of Gutenberg's printing press is on display in his original workshop in Mainz, Germany.

Technical problems

Gutenberg was born in Mainz, Germany, and trained as a goldsmith. He became very skilled in making things with metal. He invented an adjustable mold that helped him **cast** uniform pieces of metal type—each with a different letter of the alphabet on it—quickly and in large numbers. He perfected an **alloy** of tin, lead, and **antimony** that melted easily, flowed evenly, and cooled quickly. He designed an adjustable frame to hold the small letters together in lines of print that stayed straight under pressure. He improved traditional presses to apply pressure evenly across paper, and he developed a new kind of oil-based ink.

Business problems

Around 1450, Gutenberg went into partnership with a merchant, Johann Fust, who loaned him money for a printing business. Soon after, he prepared to print a Bible. This work progressed very slowly, and the partnership with Fust broke down in 1455. Because Gutenberg could not pay back the money he owed, he had to give Fust the press. Fust and his son-in-law Peter Schoeffer, who had been Gutenberg's assistant, actually finished the first printed Bible, but it is still commonly known as Gutenberg's Bible.

Print against pen

One single hand-copied Bible would take a **scribe** about four years to finish. Twenty men produced 450 Gutenberg Bibles in one year. Therefore, each one was produced ninety times faster and cost only one-tenth as much as a hand-copied version. Printing meant books were no longer only for the rich, but were for anyone who was **literate.** Instead of relying on a priest or scribe to tell them what a book said, people could read it for themselves. With new ideas and new information readily available, people began to raise new challenges to old ideas.

Most pages from the Gutenberg Bible of about 1450–55 were set with 42 lines per column. The margin decorations were added by hand.

Asian Advances

Sacred signs

By the 8th century A.D., countries like China, Korea, and Japan used printing from carved wooden blocks to reproduce religious writings and images. Rulers ordered mass production of these to bring their people good fortune and gain favor for themselves. Japan's Empress Koken (718–70) had a million charms printed to ward off smallpox—but died as the project was completed, probably of smallpox! In 983, the Chinese printed the Buddhist **scriptures** in 5,048 separate volumes, totaling 130,000 pages. Each page was printed from a separately carved block.

A problem of language

Beginning in the eleventh century, Chinese and then Korean printers tried printing using single pieces of **type** put together in different combinations. In theory, their success was a big step forward, because the older method of block-printing could only produce the same whole page over and over again.

The *Diamond Sutra,* a Buddhist scripture, is one of the oldest complete printed books, with its known date of A.D. 868.

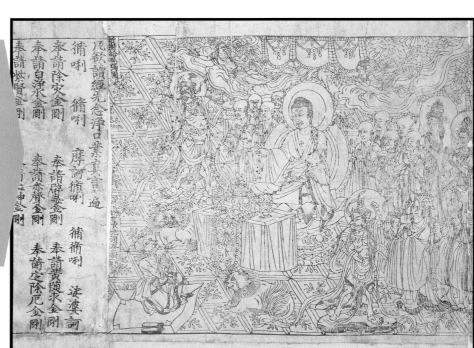

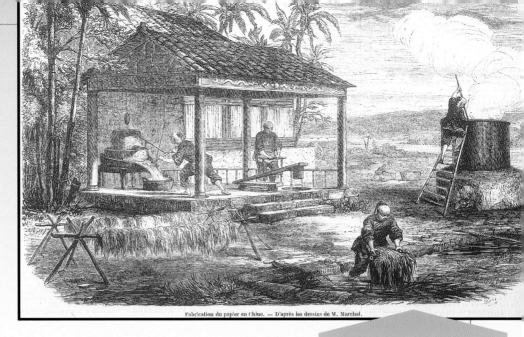

Fabrication du papier en Chine. — D'après les dessins de M. Marchal.

In practice, however, it did not help much, because the Chinese, Japanese, and Korean alphabets were made up not of just a few letters, but of thousands of characters, each standing for a thing or an idea. To choose and put together a page from a huge store of characters, and then sort them out and put them back again, took a long time. In fact, it took so long that block-printing was not usually that much slower—especially because they wanted to print the same religious books over and over again, instead of producing new ones. So this great "breakthrough" came to nothing.

This print from the nineteenth century shows people trimming and soaking bamboo to make paper in China.

PAPER

Paper was being used in China by A.D. 105. It was originally made from the inner bark of mulberry trees, which was soaked in water to make a pulp, which was then pressed into sheets and dried. Later, old rags, rope, and even fishing nets were used. Coarser papers, made from straw or wood, were also manufactured. These were not for writing, but for lanterns, fans, or wrapping. Chinese prisoners captured in Central Asia had brought the secret of paper-making to the Arab world by 795. It reached Spain by the twelfth century, and then Italy and England by the fourteenth century. Paper was less beautiful than **parchment,** which was made of animal skin. It did not last nearly as long, but was much, much cheaper.

Scribes and Scriptures

A little learning

Roman rule ended in western Europe in the fifth century A.D. Towns shrank and trade declined. About the only **literate** people left were Christian priests, trained in **monasteries.** Each large monastery had a **scriptorium,** where books were copied out by hand and novices were taught to read and write. They still used Latin, the language of the Romans, for writing and worship.

Scribes usually wrote with goose-feather **quills** and ink made from soot and oil. They could copy up to four pages a day. They wrote on **parchment** made from the scraped skins of calves, sheep, or goats. A book of 350 pages would take the skins of 200 calves. Most monastery libraries had only a few dozen books, which they loaned to other monasteries so scribes there could make their own copies.

Kings and nobles relied on scribes to keep records and accounts for them, write letters, and draw up **charters** and **treaties.** Latin was also used for all these purposes throughout Europe, whatever language was spoken locally.

Eadwine, a Canterbury monk, drew this picture of himself working on a book of Psalms in about 1150.

English achievements

In England, King Alfred (849–899) had books translated from Latin and copied by hand, in English, so more people could read them. He ordered that a **chronicle** of important events be kept in English. England also produced one of the greatest books of the Middle Ages. In 1086, William I (about 1027–87) ordered a complete survey of the kingdom. It was compiled by monks who usually spoke French, asked questions in English, and wrote in Latin. The people called the completed survey the *Domesday Book* because it reminded them of God calling everyone to account on the Day of Judgement.

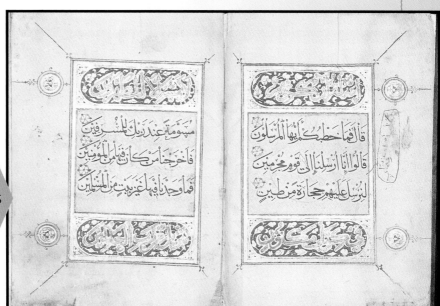

This Qur'an from the fourteenth century was handwritten in Turkey.

SACRED WORDS

Throughout the Middle Ages, Christians and Muslims were often at war. But both religions agreed that the most important books were those that recorded the words of God—the Bible and the Qur'an. Bibles and Qur'ans were written in beautiful **calligraphy** and bound in splendid covers, often decorated with gold or jewels.

In 698, Eadfrith, Bishop of Lindisfarne, an island off the English coast, began copying out the four Gospels in Latin. It took him three years. Around 950, Aeldred, a monk, wrote an Anglo-Saxon translation between the lines of Eadfrith's text. It was the first Christian **scripture** in English.

Master Caxton's Hobby

A second career

William Caxton (about 1422–91) was an English merchant who lived in Bruges in Flanders—now part of Belgium—and in Westminster, in London. Printing presses based on Gutenberg's ideas had been set up in both cities. In his spare time, Caxton translated stories from French into English. He became interested in having them printed so that more of his friends could read them.

The first book he had printed, which he had translated himself, was about the history of ancient Troy. He also printed one about chess. When he retired from business in 1476, Caxton brought a press back to England and set it up in Westminster. Over the next fifteen years, he printed about a hundred different books, including the poems of Geoffrey Chaucer and the stories of King Arthur and the Knights of the Round Table.

This illustrated page is from Chaucer's *Canterbury Tales*, printed by Caxton in 1483.

Which English?

Caxton had to decide what sort of English to print. There was no standard form. The words people used and the way they said them differed widely from region to region. Caxton himself wrote about how a storm once forced two London men to stop in Kent, only a few dozen

IMPRESSIO LIBRORVM.

Poteſt vt vna vox capi aure plurima: *Linunt ita vna ſcripta mille paginas.*

This was a print shop in Germany in the 1500s.

miles away. When one asked a local farmer's wife to sell them eggs to eat, she said that she didn't understand him because she could not speak French. He was upset because he did not speak French either! In Kent, eggs were called *eyren,* which sounds very much like their modern German name.

Caxton also noted that *"certaynly our langage now used varyeth ferre from that which was used and spoken when I was borne."* When he was printing his books, Caxton used the English of London and southeast England. As the printing industry grew, words gained regular, standard spellings, and the dialect Caxton used became the basis of the "standard English" used by educated people and on public occasions.

WHERE TO DO BUSINESS?

Caxton chose Westminster Abbey as the site for his press and bookshop because he thought its monks and visitors would be good customers. When he died, he left his business to his assistant, Wynkyn de Worde (died 1535), who moved it to Fleet Street in the city of London. De Worde thought the rich merchants and nobles there would be even better customers. For more than five centuries, Fleet Street and the area near St. Paul's Cathedral have been the home of English printing and publishing.

Bibles and Beliefs

Martin Luther

Throughout the Middle Ages, Christians in western Europe obeyed the Roman Catholic Church, headed by the pope. Its teachings were based on the Bible, but included many extra rules made by popes and councils of priests. Protestantism was a protest movement, led by a German priest, Martin Luther (1483–1546). He believed the Church was more concerned with wealth than with saving souls. Luther argued that the Bible alone taught correct Christian beliefs. This became a central idea of Protestantism. Luther translated the Bible from Latin into German so that more people could read it themselves.

The Reformation

A century earlier, Bohemian Jan Hus (about 1370–1415) and Englishman John Wycliffe (about 1320–84) had held the same ideas as Luther, but they failed to start mass movements. Printing made all the difference. The cheap Bibles first printed in Germany—as a result of Gutenberg's work—helped to spread Protestantism into neighboring France, Switzerland, Holland, and Britain. This movement became known as the Reformation because Protestants set up separate, "Reformed," churches. They refused to obey the pope and followed new ways of worshiping, based on the Bible. Protestant worship stressed study of the Bible, with preachers explaining its meaning in **sermons.**

William Tyndale (about 1494–1536) translated the New Testament into English. He knew Luther and Gutenberg's assistant, Schoeffer. Tyndale was burned at the stake in 1536 for **heresy.**

Books and beliefs

Most people were too poor to own books, but if a Protestant family did have one, it was a Bible. It was certainly the book everybody, **literate** or not, knew best, and it affected the language people used, from everyday speech to poetry. Luther's Bible also set the standard for how German should be written. In Wales, from the 1540s on, English was the language of government and law, but the appearance of a Welsh Bible in 1588 kept Welsh alive as the language of religion.

For two centuries after Luther, Europe was torn by religious wars, both between Catholics and Protestants and between different Protestant groups. One of the main reasons English people began to emigrate to America was so that they would be free to worship in the ways they chose.

This picture from a nineteenth-century edition of Foxe's *Book of Martyrs* shows two Protestant bishops, Latimer and Ridley, being burned in 1555, during the reign of the Catholic Queen Mary I.

BEST SELLERS

Religion was the main subject of many of the most famous books printed in this period. After the Bible, the most popular book in England at the time was Foxe's *Book of Martyrs* (first published in 1554), about Protestants who had died for their beliefs. John Milton's long poem *Paradise Lost* explains how Satan, originally an angel, was thrown out of heaven. John Bunyan's *The Pilgrim's Progress* told how its hero, Christian, came through many dangers and evils to reach heaven at last.

Printing the World

Secret knowledge

Printing made books cheaper and more plentiful, but this did not mean the information in them was more accurate. This was even more true of maps. Before printing was developed, maps were drawn by hand. It was easy to control how many were produced and circulated. Trading countries such as Portugal and the Netherlands grew rich bringing spices from Asia. They did not want other countries to know their sea-routes to Asia, so they tried to keep this information to themselves. After Englishman Francis Drake sailed around the world (1577–80), his **logbook** was kept top secret, and no mention of his adventure appeared in print for over ten years. Long after printing developed, seamen continued to depend on hand-drawn maps as being more reliable, easier to keep updated, and secret.

Profit before truth

Early printed maps were made using engraved blocks of wood. After about 1550, the wooden blocks were replaced by copper printing plates. These were very expensive to prepare, so printers often refused to throw them away—even after new geographical discoveries. They often just kept printing the same old maps. At times, they even sold them next to newer ones that showed different information. A Portuguese ship sailed around Africa into the Indian Ocean in 1497, but maps ignoring this sea route to India were still being sold in 1570.

This nineteenth-century map by the Flemish mapmaker Gerardus Mercator (1512–94) helped to change our way of looking at the world, by treating it as an exploded globe.

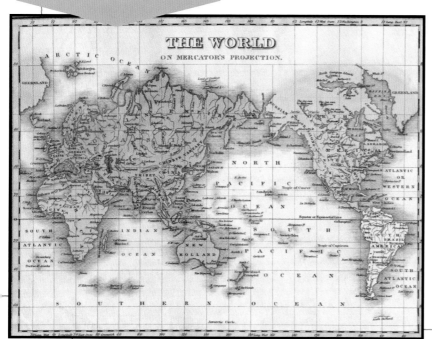

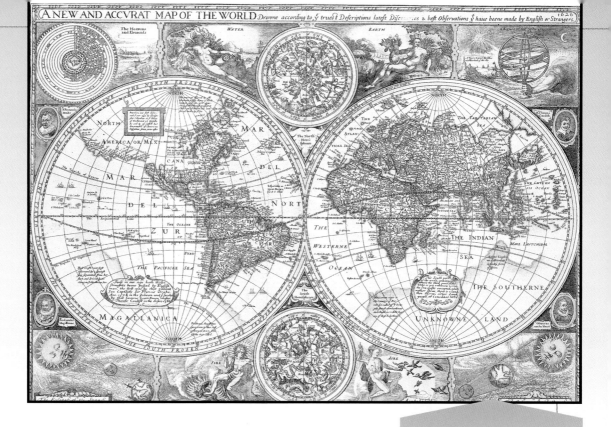

This English world map, first drawn in around 1610, pays tribute to Drake and other explorers.

Naming America

Italian-born Amerigo Vespucci (1454–1512) sold supplies to Christopher Columbus before making his own voyage to explore the coast of South America. He wrote a letter in Italian describing his travels, which was later printed in Latin.

In 1507, Martin Waldseemüller (1470–1518), a German amateur printer, published a description of the world. It included a large map printed from twelve wooden blocks, which drew on the Latin version of Amerigo Vespucci's letter. It was Waldseemüller who decided that the newly discovered continent described by Vespucci should be called "America" in his honor. Later, he decided that Vespucci did not deserve the credit after all. He left out the name "America" on his next three maps, but it was too late. He had already sold 1,000 copies of the first version, so the name stuck.

Read All About It!

Before newspapers were produced, merchants and bankers needed a way to find out what was going on so they could run their businesses. They paid for regular "intelligencers" or "courants," handwritten reports of the latest news from important cities.

Germany and France lead

The world's first newspaper was the *Relation,* published in Strasbourg, France, in 1609, although a close rival is the German *Avisa Relation*. The *Leipziger Journal,* launched as a weekly in 1660, soon became the world's first daily newspaper. The *Wiener Zeitung,* first published in Vienna, Austria, in 1703, is the oldest newspaper still being printed.

This 1643 issue of a weekly paper published in London carries news of the British civil war.

England catches up

In the 1620s, Dutch printers began to send "corantos" over to England, which were cheaply printed pamphlets of foreign news. During Britain's civil wars (1642–49), the weakened government could no longer control what was being printed. Thousands of pamphlets were made, all putting forward different political and religious points of view. By the late 1600s, printed news-sheets were being circulated regularly in the London coffee houses, where men met for business. Their most important news was about ships' cargoes. London's first regular daily newspaper was the *Daily Courant,* published 1702–35. Newspapers soon appeared in **provincial** cities, including Norwich, Bristol, Worcester, and Exeter. By 1760, there were four London dailies; by 1790, there were fourteen. The number of provincial papers, usually published weekly, rose from 35 in 1760 to 150 by 1821.

The London Malignants difarmed, (89)
Fifty thoufand pounds to be raifed,
The Lord Capels Forces difperfed,
The Cavaliers from Glocefter repulfed.

Numb. 12

Mercurius Civicus.

LONDONS

INTELLIGENCER:

OR,

Truth impartially related from thence to the whole Kingdome, to prevent mif-information.

From *Friday August* 11. to *Thursday August* 17. 1643.

Oth Houfes of Parliament and the City of *London,* have a long time been much indangered through the Plots and confpiracies of many malignant Inhabitants in that City, the Suburbs, and parts adjacent; notwithftanding which, that City, which in many other things of great confequence to this Nation both in former and latter time, hath afforded
M

America

The American colonies' earliest newspaper, *Publick Occurrences,* appeared in 1690 and was banned by the government after only one issue! In 1704, Scottish printer John Campbell began publishing a weekly *Boston Newsletter.* He took two-thirds of its contents from London papers, filling the rest with shipping news, law and court proceedings, extracts from sermons, and short stories about storms, deaths, or other dramatic events.

Power of the press

By the nineteenth century, many governments were run by elected leaders rather than royal rulers. Newspaper reports of speeches and debates became an important way for voters to find out politicians' views. Newspapers' **editorials** and letters pages gave politicians feedback from public opinion about events and policies. Many political parties linked themselves with certain newspapers. Newspapers also investigated **scandals** and injustices, which people then expected governments to correct.

By the nineteenth century, magazines were also widely circulated. This illustration from *Harper's New Monthly Magazine* shows how it was produced in New York in 1865. Notice the many women working there.

Prominent Printers

Before the twentieth century, printing was the main form of communication. Many famous printers were very successful and became rich and powerful.

Inventor

Boston-born Benjamin Franklin (1706–90) invented a lightning rod, bifocal lenses, and a stove. He also helped to write the United States Declaration of Independence and Constitution. But before all those achievements, he was a printer. In 1724–26, Franklin worked in London, the greatest center for printing in the English-speaking world. When he returned to America, he won the contract to print paper money for Pennsylvania. He later printed official documents for New Jersey, Maryland, and Delaware as well.

In 1729, he started a newspaper, the *Pennsylvania Gazette.* In each year between 1732 and 1757, he published an edition of *Poor Richard's Almanack,* a practical book containing **astronomical** information and farming notes, mixed in with rhymes and jokes. Franklin also set up Philadelphia's first library, and started an academy that became the University of Pennsylvania.

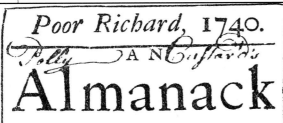

Poor Richard, 1740.

AN Cuffard's

Almanack

For the Year of Chrift

1740,

Being LEAP YEAR.

And makes fince the Creation Years.
By the Account of the Eaftern *Greeks* 7248
By the Latin Church, when ☉ ent. ♈ 6939
By the Computation of *W. W.* 5749
By the *Roman* Chronology 5689
By the *Jewifh* Rabbies 5501

Wherein is contained,

The Lunations, Eclipfes, Judgment of the Weather, Spring Tides, Planets Motions & mutual Afpects, Sun and Moon's Rifing and Setting, Length of Days, Time of High Water, Fairs, Courts, and obfervable Days.

Fitted to the Latitude of Forty Degrees, and a Meridian of Five Hours Weft from *London,* but may without fenfible Error, ferve all the adjacent Places, even from *Newfoundland* to *South-Carolina.*

By RICHARD SAUNDERS, Philom.

PHILADELPHIA:
Printed and fold by *B. FRANKLIN,* at the New Printing-Office near the Market.

Benjamin Franklin's *Poor Richard's Almanack* became the only other book besides the Bible in many colonial American homes.

Writer

Samuel Richardson (1689–1761) had a business near Fleet Street, the center of London's printing trade. He produced books, magazines, advertising posters, letterheads, and business cards. In 1723, he took over printing a political newspaper, the *True Briton,* and in 1733 began printing for the House of Commons. In 1739–40, he wrote and published a novel, *Pamela,* which was widely praised. In France, it was made into a play. Another novel, *Clarissa,* was translated into French, Dutch, and German. In 1754–55, Richardson served as master of the **Stationers' Company,** helping to run the country's printing business.

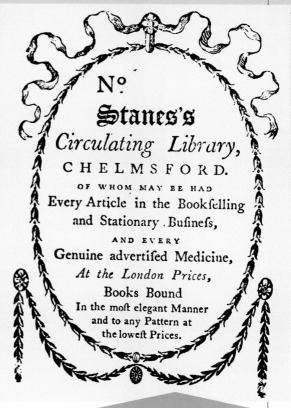

No.
Stanes's
Circulating Library,
C H E L M S F O R D.
OF WHOM MAY BE HAD
Every Article in the Bookselling and Stationary . Business,
AND EVERY
Genuine advertised Medicine,
At the London Prices,
Books Bound
In the most elegant Manner and to any Pattern at the lowest Prices.

This eighteenth-century English printer sold stationery and medicines, as well as typesetting, binding, and lending out books.

Family businesses

Luke Hansard (1752–1828) took on responsibility for printing for the House of Commons when he was only 22. This work became the family business. His son Thomas (1776–1833) wrote a history and handbook of printing. The reports of House of Commons proceedings became known simply as *Hansard,* and are still called this today.

Thomas De La Rue (1793–1866) began by making ladies' summer bonnets out of paper, and went on to print headed stationery, playing cards, checks, and stamps. Warren De La Rue (1815–89) invented an envelope-making machine and pioneered astronomical photography in his leisure time. Sir Thomas De La Rue (1849–1911) made the firm a worldwide business, printing stamps and bank notes for many foreign countries.

The Rise of the Writer

Benjamin Franklin and Samuel Richardson were businessmen first and writers second. But as more people learned to read and write, and had spare time to read for pleasure, it became possible to make a full-time living just from writing.

Fame . . .

Samuel Johnson (1709–84) lived in poverty for years before becoming famous for compiling the first true dictionary of the English language (1755). Later, the English poets Percy Shelley (1792–1822), John Keats (1795–1821), and Lord Byron (1788–1824) all found fame, despite dying young. Novelist Jane Austen (1775–1817) was praised by Sir Walter Scott (1771–1832), a best-selling writer of the time, but lived a quiet country life. Jane Austen's novels are still widely read and have been adapted into TV dramas and films.

Alice in Wonderland was originally written in a diary, with pictures by the author, Lewis Carroll.

In 1783, Noah Webster (1758–1843), creator of the first dictionary of American English, published the *American Spelling Book*. It sold about 100,000,000 copies over the following century. William Holmes McGuffey's "readers," compiled from 1853 on to teach reading to Americans, sold over 125 million copies.

. . . and fortune

Writing novels raised Charles Dickens (1812–70) and W. M. Thackeray (1811–63) to fame and fortune. Anthony Trollope (1815–82) worked as a post office official but wrote from 5:30 until breakfast each morning before he went to work. In this way, he wrote 47 books to raise extra money to support his family. Washington Irving (1783–1859), creator of "Rip Van Winkle," was the first American writer to become famous outside the United States. Mark Twain (1835–1910)—printer, riverboat pilot, gold miner, editor—drew on his American adventures in humorous novels that made him popular on both sides of the Atlantic. Best-selling authors of the twentieth century include American child-care expert Dr. Benjamin Spock and English mystery author Agatha Christie.

This is the American author Mark Twain on the day he received an honorary degree from Oxford University.

FOR YOUNGER READERS

Some of the world's best-selling books have been written mainly for younger readers. They include Lewis Carroll's *Alice in Wonderland* (1865) and Beatrix Potter's *The Tale of Peter Rabbit* (1902). Enid Blyton (1897–1968), creator of "Noddy" and "The Famous Five," wrote over 700 books, which have sold over 100 million copies in 1,000 translations. Other best-selling children's authors of the century have included the creators of *The Cat in the Hat* (Dr. Seuss—United States), *Tintin* (Hergé—Belgium), and *Asterix* (Renée Goscinny—France).

Prints, Posters, Packaging

Profitable prints

English artist William Hogarth (1697–1764) trained as an **engraver.** He wanted to be a painter, but knew that paintings often took a long time to complete and even longer to sell. Hogarth became successful by painting scenes of London life and then turning them into engravings. Instead of selling one expensive picture to one buyer, he could sell hundreds of cheap printed copies to many buyers. In 1735, he persuaded Parliament to pass a law allowing artists to **copyright** their pictures, just like authors did with their books.

Publishers found that books of prints showing beautiful natural views, the homes of the wealthy, and scenes of foreign travel all sold well. Around 1800, the English cartoonists Gillray, Rowlandson, and Cruikshank produced hundreds of **caricatures** attacking the politicians and fashionable leaders of society.

Prints of ruins were popular, since scenic, picturesque views were very fashionable.

J. Wooding sculp.

CASTLE ACRE MONASTERY, in NORFOLK.

Print for profits

As populations, incomes, and **literacy** rates all grew rapidly in the nineteenth century, huge printing opportunities opened up. Businesses needed supplies of headed bills, receipts, **ledgers,** and labels. The increased use of paper money produced a need for banknotes that were difficult to **forge.** Railways, steamships, and bus companies needed tickets. More and more foods and medicines were sold in sealed packets that carried printed information or advertising. In 1840, Britain issued the world's first prepaid sticky postage stamps. Other countries quickly copied the idea. From the 1880s on, there was a need for telephone directories. Specialized businesses opened to produce items such as tickets numbered in sequence or invitation cards printed in gold.

POSTERS, POLITICS, AND PLEASURE

The first posters were government announcements of new laws, taxes, or chances to join the army. As more people could read and vote, political parties began to use posters to get support at elections. Theaters used posters to tell audiences about their changing programs. In France, clubs, restaurants, exhibitions, and galleries employed artists to design posters with pictures to attract customers. Posters by artists such as Jules Chéret (1836–1932), Henri de Toulouse-Lautrec (1864–1901), and Alphonse Mucha (1860–1939) are now regarded as important works of art.

THE MANAGERS OF THE NEW
IPSWICH THEATRE,

Beg most respectfully to inform their Patrons and the public in general, that they have, at a very considerable outlay, completed their arrangements, and having also engaged some of the best Vocal Performers, in addition to their Establishment, intend opening their Theatre on the 31st inst., with the popular Comedy of

WHIG GRATITUDE :
OR,
A NEW WAY TO PAY OLD DEBTS.

In which the celebrated Performers will introduce the following New Songs, written entirely for the occasion, and of which the Managers have the entire Copyright.

BILLY BLOATER,
ALIAS,
THE MITY MAN.
"Did I not Soap the knowing ones."
"Could I refuse, when he married my sisters."
"I'm badly off, for Tin, my friend."

SHUFFLING JOHNNY.
"Oh Give me, Give me, Burton Ale."
"I've Butter, Cheese, and Lard in Store."

Allen Broadbrim
"The Renegade."
"Can I not tell a dirty tale."

JERRY SMOOTHFACE.
"I'd golden Hopes in Railway Shares,
Alas! they now are gone."

HOOKEY GEORGE.
"We are all in the Hadleigh Line."

TOMMY DYE.
"My Mother would not give consent."

Messrs. Gaslight & Glyster
Will also introduce the pathetic Duet of
"Farewell to the Ward of St. Clement for ever."

To conclude with the celebrated Hornpipe called the

JACKALL's JIG
By LOTTO HENSERO

One of the Black Monkey tribe, who will be exhibited for a few nights only, as his Proprietor has determined to travel with him in a Puppet-show, with a collection of other animals of a similar nature.

The Managers beg also to state that they have another Play in Rehearsal, called
THE THIMBLE-RIG COMPANY.
The particulars of which will be printed in a few days.

Ipswich: Smith, Brown, _____, Printers to the Establishment.

Cheap posters using many different **typefaces** helped **provincial** printers earn regular income.

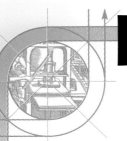

Better and Better, Faster and Faster

How printing spread

There were printers in over 100 European cities and towns by 1480, and in over 230 by 1500. By then, around a thousand printing presses had produced several million books. During the sixteenth century, Germany produced 45,000 different titles, France 38,000, and England 10,000. Italy and the Netherlands also had important printing industries. This growth opened up the world to people who had previously known little beyond their own towns or villages. The rapid spread of new ideas, particularly about religion and politics, changed Europe's history forever.

New print

The earliest printed books were made to look as much like traditional hand-copied books as possible. As printed books became more popular, though, printers designed new **typefaces** especially for printing. Two of the most famous are roman (1470) and italic (1501). These were far easier to read than the earliest kind of print, which imitated handwriting.

The Stanhope press, invented in 1800, could print much bigger sheets than earlier presses, and was much faster.

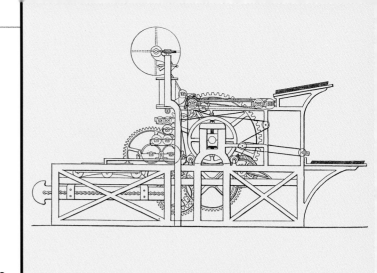

Faster

In Gutenberg's day, a hardworking printer could turn out about 300 pages a day, but he had to open the press to insert each new sheet of blank paper. In 1620, Dutch printer Willem Blaeu introduced a **counterweighted** press that opened automatically as each sheet was printed. A printer could now run off 150 copies an hour.

Shade and color

Early printers could not make gradual tones, shading from black, through gray, to white. But in 1642, Colonel Ludwig von Siegen of Hesse in Germany invented a method using copper plates. These were usually roughened to hold printing ink, but when smoothed and cleaned of ink, gave a white or gray effect. This process, called "mezzotint" from the Italian for "half-tint," can show fine differences of light and shade. It was used for printing portraits and works of art. Full-color printing, mixing red, yellow, and blue inks to produce a wide range of colors, was also developed in Germany in 1719.

Faster presses

In 1800, the English Lord Stanhope invented a printing press made of iron, rather than wood. This could print much bigger sheets at a rate of 250 an hour. Between 1810 and 1816, Friedrich Koenig (1774–1833), a German working in London, perfected a steam-powered printing press that could print both sides of a sheet at once, at a rate of 1,000 copies an hour. By 1850, rotary presses that printed from a circular drum, not a flat sheet of **type,** could turn out 15,000 copies an hour.

Back to Beautiful Books

Now that steam-powered machinery could print books on paper made from wood pulp, and bind them in cotton or cardboard covers, many more people could afford them. The books themselves, however, were not lovely to look at or handle. Cheap ink faded. Cheap paper cracked. Cheap bindings and covers were easily torn or fell apart.

Crusade for beauty

When he was in his 50s, English artist and poet William Morris (1834–96) decided to revive the art of making fine books. He was already rich enough to finance this hobby, and was well-qualified for the task. Morris was famous for designing wallpapers, textiles, and furniture. He was also a talented **calligrapher,** an expert on English literature, and a collector of old books and manuscripts. Morris had strong views about art and work. He believed that beautiful things would be produced only by craftsmen who enjoyed their work and took pride in it.

This Kelmscott Chaucer is on display at William Morris's childhood home, Water House, at Walthamstow, East London.

Morris founded the Kelmscott Press in 1891 in his house at Hammersmith, London, and printed 52 different titles. His greatest achievement was an edition of Chaucer's *Canterbury Tales*. Morris himself designed the **typeface,** based on fifteenth-century writing styles. His friend, artist Edward Burne-Jones, did the illustrations. Each page was meant to be as pleasing as a picture.

Private presses

The Kelmscott Press inspired the founding of other private printing presses on both sides of the Atlantic. Their aim was not to make money, but to present the best of literature in the best possible way. C. R. Ashbee, a follower of Morris, took over his printing press and founded Essex House Press (1898–1910) in London's East End. Charles Ricketts' Vale Press (1896–1903) printed all of Shakespeare's works in 39 volumes. French artist Lucien Pissarro took over the Vale Press **types** for his Eragny Press, which introduced elegant patterned paper bindings. The Doves Press (1901–20) produced a splendid five-volume Bible for use in churches.

20TH-CENTURY PRINTERS AND TYPOGRAPHERS

America's greatest book designer, Bruce Rogers (1870–1957), created the Centaur typeface used by the Metropolitan Museum of Art, and he also worked with Harvard University Press. D. B. Updike (1860–1941), a follower of Morris, founded the Merrymount Press and taught printing history at Harvard. In San Francisco, Edwin and Robert Grabhorn printed books for the Book Club of California. English **engraver** Eric Gill (1882–1940) is probably best remembered as the designer of the typeface known as Gill sans serif.

This is a sentence written in

CENTAUR TYPEFACE

designed by Bruce Rogers in 1915.

Pages Without Printing

Invention by accident

In 1904, New York printer Ira Rubel noticed by chance that a rubber pad could transfer the image from an inked metal printing plate onto paper—and make a better picture than the actual plate could. This led to the process of offset printing, in which the image or text is transferred—offset—from a zinc printing plate to a rubber-covered cylinder and then rolled onto paper. This process is faster and cheaper than any earlier methods. Modern offset machines can print 70,000 newspapers an hour, using reels holding over 12 miles (20 kilometers) of paper.

Invention by design

Setting **type** into page-size "forms" or frames was a skilled craft. The **compositor** used a keyboard like a typewriter to set up lines of type for a metal mold. Then, in 1939, American William Heubner invented a process called photosetting, using a machine that projected characters onto film at the tap of a key. By 1954, improved photosetting machines could set 1,000 characters a minute. In 1957, English publisher Penguin photoset a book for the first time.

These typesetters worked in a newspaper office around 1900. The work was skilled, clean, and paid well.

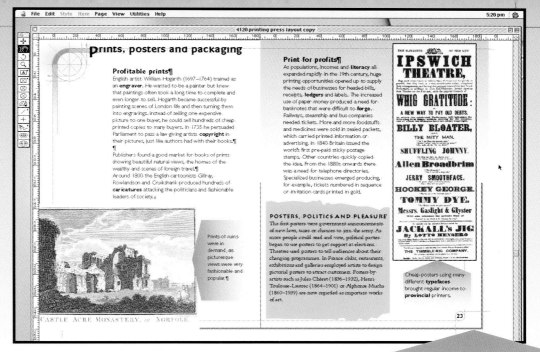

Electronic publishing

In 1947, the American Fairchild Corporation developed an electronic scanner, which beamed a picture onto a spinning drum. Signals were sent to a cutter that **engraved** a copy of the image on the printing surface. Computer-controlled systems were developed in Germany in the 1960s. In 1982, the Postscript software language allowed printers to make up pages of text and pictures electronically. In 1985, Pagemaker™ software adapted the process for personal computers.

Many authors abandoned typewriters to deliver books on disks. By the 1990s, journalists equipped with a laptop, digital camera, and cell phone could use satellite communications to beam words and images from anywhere in the world straight to their home news desk and into the newspaper's mainframe computer. Nowadays, newspapers and books are sent between computer terminals by electronic pulses before the presses finally roll and print them on paper.

In March 2000, best-selling author Stephen King published a short story straight onto the Internet. Readers paid $2 to download it, bypassing the printing process altogether. Could this be another turning point for printing?

Modern page layout is done with specialized computer programs such as QuarkXPress™, which runs on Apple Mac and PC computers.

Important Dates

105	Paper known to be in use in China
698–700	*Lindisfarne Gospel* copied by Bishop Eadfrith
795	Paper-making process known in Baghdad, Iraq
983	Chinese print complete Buddhist **scriptures**
1086	*Domesday Book* compiled in England
1455	Gutenberg Bible printed
1468	Death of Johann Gutenberg
1470	Roman **typeface** introduced
1476	William Caxton brings printing to England
1501	Italic typeface introduced
1507	Waldseemüller names America
1522	Luther translates New Testament from Greek and Hebrew into Germa
1525	William Tyndale's English translation of the New Testament is printed in Cologne, Germany
1534	Luther translates entire Bible into German
1554	Foxe's *Book of Martyrs* published
1588	Bible printed in Welsh
1609	World's first newspaper published in Strasbourg, France
1615	*Frankfurter Journal* published
1620	Blaeu's **counterweighted** press introduced
1642	Mezzotint process invented
1702	*Daily Courant,* London's first regular daily newspaper, published
1703	*Wiener Zeitung* published in Vienna, Austria
1704	*Boston Newsletter* published in America
1719	Full-color printing pioneered in Germany
1732	Benjamin Franklin begins publishing *Poor Richard's Almanack*
1735	Hogarth persuades Parliament to pass Copyright Act
1755	Samuel Johnson's *Dictionary* completed
1774	Luke Hansard prints the debates of the British House of Commons
1783	Noah Webster publishes *American Spelling Book*
1799	Machine for making paper as a roll, not sheets, invented in France
1816	Koenig steam-powered rotary press perfected
1840	Penny Black postage stamp issued in Britain
1850	Rotary presses produce 15,000 copies per hour
1891	William Morris founds the Kelmscott Press
1904	Ira Rubel pioneers offset printing
1939	William Heubner pioneers photo-typesetting
1982	Electronic page-making process introduced
2000	Stephen King publishes short story straight onto Internet

Glossary

alloy mixture of metals

antimony poisonous, silvery-white metal used in casting type

astronomical relating to the science of the movements of stars and planets

calligraphy art of beautiful writing

caricature cartoon exaggerating faces and features

cast to make an object by pouring hot metal into a mold

charter legal document granting rights or privileges

chronicle official record of important events

compositor person who sets type into pages ready for printing

copyright legal ownership of the right to reproduce a book or work of art

counterweight weight suspended near the end of a moving part of a machine that keeps the machine balanced and easier to work with

editorial part of a newspaper written by the people who run it, giving their opinions on the news

engraver someone who carves designs into printing plates

forge to make an illegal copy of something valuable, such as a bank note

heresy having religious beliefs that do not agree with church teachings

ledger large book for keeping accounts of money earned and paid out

literate able to read and write

logbook official record of a voyage kept by the captain of a ship

monastery shared home of a community of monks or other religious group

parchment fine writing surface made by scraping and cleaning animal skin

provincial relating to areas outside a country's capital or other large cities

quill pen made from a bird's feather cut to a point

scandal event considered by many to be disgraceful or offensive

scribe person who makes a living by copying documents or writing letters for others

scriptorium writing room of a monastery

scripture sacred writings of a religion

sermon talk given by a church leader and based on the Bible, to explain how Christians should behave

Stationers' Company London-based organization chartered in 1557 to control training and production in the printing trade; its powers could be used to suppress books the government disapproved of

treaty formal agreement, often between two countries

type small block of metal cast in relief to bear a letter or mark used in printing

typeface set of type made to a particular style or size

More Books to Read

Burch, Joann J. *Fine Print: A Story about Johann Gutenberg*. Minneapolis, Minn.: The Lerner Publishing Group, 1991.

Steffens, Bradley. *The Printing Press: Ideas into Type*. San Diego, Calif.: Lucent Books, 1990.

Index